SportsZone Biographies

SERENA WILLIAMS

BY ANTHONY K. HEWSON

SportsZone

An Imprint of Abdo Publishing
abdobooks.com

abdobooks.com

Published by Abdo Publishing, a division of ABDO, PO Box 398166, Minneapolis, Minnesota 55439.

Printed in the United States of America, North Mankato, Minnesota.
052023
092023

THIS BOOK CONTAINS RECYCLED MATERIALS

Cover Photo: Elsa/Getty Images Sport/Getty Images
Interior Photos: Clive Brunskill/Getty Images Sport/Getty Images, 5, 17, 24; Quinn Rooney/Getty Images Sport/Getty Images, 7; Paul Harris/Online USA/Getty Images Sport/Getty Images, 9; Timothy A. Clary/AFP/Getty Images, 11; Jamie Squire/Allsport/Getty Images Sport/Getty Images, 12; Clive Brunskill/Hulton Archive/Getty Images, 15; Ezra Shaw/Getty Images Sport/Getty Images, 19; David Goldman/AP Images, 21; Mark J. Terrill/AP Images, 23; Kena Betancur/AFP/Getty Images, 26; Sarah Stier/Getty Images Sport/Getty Images, 29

Editors: Steph Giedd and Charlie Beattie
Series Designer: Karli Kruse

LIBRARY OF CONGRESS CONTROL NUMBER: 2022949083

Publisher's Cataloging-in-Publication Data

Names: Hewson, Anthony K., author.
Title: Serena Williams / by Anthony K. Hewson
Description: Minneapolis, Minnesota: Abdo Publishing Company, 2024 | Series: SportsZone biographies | Includes online resources and index.
Identifiers: ISBN 9781098291716 (lib. bdg.) | ISBN 9781098278267 (ebook)
Subjects: LCSH: Williams, Serena, 1981--Juvenile literature. | Tennis players--Biography --Juvenile literature. | Women tennis players--Biography--Juvenile literature. | African American women tennis players--Biography--Juvenile literature. | Professional athletes--Biography--Juvenile literature.
Classification: DDC 796.092--dc23

TABLE OF CONTENTS

Chapter One

BORN TO BE GREAT

The biggest moment in Serena Williams's career came against her toughest opponent. It was also her most familiar opponent: her sister Venus. The siblings were each other's first playing partners. Now they were both legends of the sport.

The stage was the 2017 Australian Open. The sisters had met in eight Grand Slam singles finals before. But this one was different. Younger sister Serena was on the edge of history.

Serena had won 22 Grand Slam singles titles. That tied her for the most in the Open Era, the period beginning in 1968 when professionals were allowed to enter Grand Slam tournaments. A victory for Serena tonight would move her past the great Steffi Graf for the record. This was no time to

Serena Williams celebrates a point during the 2017 Australian Open.

Chapter Two

THE SERENA SLAM

The Williams sisters were taking the tennis world by storm. It was hard enough to beat one of them. But to make it even harder, they started teaming up.

Before they started winning Grand Slam singles titles, they were doubles champions. Eighteen-year-old Venus and 17-year-old Serena won the 1999 French Open women's doubles title. The sisters played an aggressive style that made them fierce opponents.

Serena ended the 1999 season by taking the next step as a singles player, too. At that year's US Open, she stormed through the field with upset after upset. Her precise serve and coverage of the court helped her march through a powerful field. In four consecutive matches, Williams beat top players Kim Clijsters, Conchita Martinez, Monica Seles, and defending champion Lindsay Davenport.

As doubles partners, Venus, *left*, and Serena Williams won 14 Grand Slam titles together.

Williams kisses her trophy after defeating Martina Hingis to win the 1999 US Open.

That set up a meeting with Martina Hingis, who was the number one player in the world. The 18-year-old Hingis was also a teenage sensation, but Williams was the one to seize the moment. After winning the first set 6–3, Williams outlasted Hingis in the second set. With the two tied 6–6, Williams took the tiebreak by a 7–4 score to lift the trophy. On the final point, Williams demonstrated the power game that was quickly becoming her signature. She hammered a wide serve that sent Hingis lunging to return it. Then Williams followed up with two strong backhands.

After returning the first one, Hingis sent the second one long. With the win, Williams became the first Black woman since 1958 to win a Grand Slam singles title.

SUCCESSES AND SETBACKS

Williams battled through injuries over the next few seasons. One tournament where she was healthy was the 2000 Summer Olympics in Sydney, Australia. There she teamed up with Venus for the women's doubles competition. The pair cruised to the gold medal. In the final, they lost only two games.

Williams was still struggling with injuries when 2002 started. She had to pull out of the Australian Open in January. That ended up creating one of the great what-ifs in tennis history. Winning the Australian Open, the French Open, Wimbledon, and the US Open in one calendar year is known as a "Grand Slam." Only three women had done it entering 2002. Because she didn't win in Australia, Williams couldn't add her name to the list that year. But she still dominated the rest of the season.

FAST FACT

Serena Williams was the second Black woman to win a Grand Slam title. Althea Gibson was the first, winning Wimbledon in 1958. Gibson had a successful and historic career as the first Black player to compete at the US championships. That was what the tournament was called before it became the US Open in 1968.

FAST FACT

Williams started displaying her unique sense of fashion in 2002. At the US Open she wore an all-black bodysuit for one match. It was a far cry from the tennis skirts that women had traditionally worn while competing.

Serena met Venus in all three of the other 2002 major finals. And Serena won all three in straight sets. Along the way, Serena was ranked number one for the first time in July 2002. She became the second Black woman to achieve the top ranking. The first was her sister, Venus.

The sisters met again at the Australian Open in January 2003. This time the match was tighter. Serena ultimately won 7–6, 3–6, 6–4. With the win, Serena became the holder of all four major titles. It wasn't a Grand Slam since they had not all come in the same year. But only five other women had ever held all four titles at the same time. The press dubbed her feat the "Serena Slam." It was proof that the 21-year-old was without a doubt the top player in the world.

Williams delivers a serve during the 2003 French Open.

Chapter Three

RETURN TO NUMBER ONE

Serena Williams's Grand Slam streak ended at the 2003 French Open before she repeated her title at Wimbledon. However, a quadriceps injury that needed surgery ended her year. Injuries became the story for Williams once again. She had to pull out of the 2004 Olympics in Athens, Greece. Then she barely played in 2005 and 2006, though she did win the 2005 Australian Open. Still, at one point her ranking fell to 140th. Williams would have to fight hard to regain her place at the top.

Before the 2007 Australian Open, Williams said her goal was to get back to the top ranking in the world. Not many believed she could do it. Former player Pat Cash called the idea "deluded." Even Williams's sponsor, Nike, threatened to drop her as a client if she didn't play better.

In 2003 Williams signed Nike's largest endorsement contract for a female athlete at the time. It was for five years and $40 million.

FAST FACT

The women's tour officially began tracking serve speeds in 2008. In 2013 Williams clocked a serve at a speed of 128.7 miles per hour (207.1 km/h).

That meant the match was over. Williams had lost.

She faced stiff penalties for the incident. Williams was fined $82,000, the biggest fine in tennis history. She was also placed on probation. If she had any more discipline issues over the next year, she would be barred from the 2010 US Open and face bigger fines.

A SCARY INJURY

Williams avoided further on-court behavior problems, but she still missed out on the 2010 US Open. Before the tournament, she stepped on a piece of broken glass. The injury kept her out of the tournament. But an even more terrifying health scare happened in 2011. A pulmonary embolism, which is a blood clot in her lung, hospitalized and nearly killed her. Williams returned in time to make it to the fourth round at Wimbledon, but she was once again sliding down the rankings. Even though she reached the 2011 US Open final, Williams dropped to 175th in the world in July 2011. The following year she lost in the first round of the French Open. It was the first time she had been knocked out in the opening round of a Grand Slam tournament.

However, Williams charged back. She won Wimbledon for the fifth time in 2012. Then she won her first Olympic singles

Williams stretches to reach a ball in her comeback win at the US Open final against Victoria Azarenka.

gold medal at the Summer Games in London. Williams capped off her comeback with a dramatic effort in the US Open final. Victoria Azarenka of Belarus built a 5–3 lead in the third set and then got to match point. Though Azarenka was serving, Williams battled back to win the game. Then she won three more to claim the championship.

The next year, Williams vaulted back to number one again. She won the French Open for the first time in 11 years and then repeated at the US Open. After her success in both tournaments, at 31, she was the oldest player ever to hold the top spot. And Williams was far from done.

Chapter Four

GOING OUT ON TOP

By 2014 Serena Williams had seen many peaks and valleys in her career. She'd battled injuries, depression, and life-threatening conditions but was still one of the best in her sport for nearly two decades. And she still had more to give.

She capped that 2014 season by repeating as US Open champion. It was the start of another incredible run. Williams won the Australian Open for the sixth time to open 2015.

Before the next Grand Slam tournament, Williams returned to the event at Indian Wells, California, in March. It was an emotional moment. Williams had last played in the event in 2001. That year she won it but did so through tears after hearing racist taunts from the crowd in the final. Both Serena and Venus vowed never to play at Indian Wells again.

Williams celebrates a point during her return to play at Indian Wells in California after a 14-year protest.

This time, the crowd gave her a one-minute standing ovation as she entered the court for her first match.

A win at the French Open that June gave her at least three wins in all four major tournaments. And when she won Wimbledon at age 33 in July, she became the oldest woman to win a major singles title.

The Wimbledon win also gave her a second career "Serena Slam." Another win a few weeks later at the 2015 US Open could secure the coveted season Grand Slam. No player had done that since Steffi Graf in 1988. And a win in New York would also tie Graf's Open Era record of 22 Grand Slam titles.

Williams entered the tournament as the top seed and rolled to the semifinals. There she met unseeded Italian Roberta Vinci. Williams won the first set 6–2, but Vinci bounced back to win the next two sets 6–4, 6–4. After the

Williams was ranked No. 1 in the world for a total of 319 weeks.

win, Vinci apologized to the New York crowd that was hoping to see Williams make even more history.

It took until the following summer for Williams to finally match Graf. After tough losses in both the 2016 Australian Open and French Open finals, Williams put together a dominant Wimbledon performance. She lost only one set in the entire tournament. Later that year, Williams reached 186 straight weeks as the world's number one player. That tied another record set by Graf.

FOR ALL TIME

The following January, Serena defeated Venus at the Australian Open to win her 23rd major title. The feat put her alone at the top. And the accomplishment was made even more incredible by news that came out later that year. In April Williams announced that she was 20 weeks pregnant. That meant she had been carrying her baby while breaking the record in Australia. That September, she and her husband, Alexis Ohanian, welcomed their daughter Alexis Olympia Ohanian Jr.

Complications from the pregnancy kept Williams from returning to tennis. She suffered

FAST FACT

Williams met internet businessman Alexis Ohanian in 2015. Ohanian is best known for cofounding the website Reddit. They married in 2017.

a second life-threatening pulmonary embolism. Williams was also open about suffering from postpartum depression. She eventually played a match in late December and returned to major competition at the 2018 French Open, reaching the fourth round. Williams was 37 years old. But she still had the desire to compete at the highest level.

Williams's daughter Alexis Olympia snaps a picture of her mom during the 2022 US Open.

Once again, she silenced any doubters. In July 2018, Williams reached the Wimbledon final, where she lost to German Angelique Kerber. Williams also reached the US Open final only to lose to Naomi Osaka.

THE EVOLUTION OF SERENA

Williams was also building a full life off the court. Long interested in fashion, she now had her own clothing line. She had also championed many causes centered on social and racial justice. And her charity work saw her aiding everyone from residents in her hometown of Compton, California, to people in Africa.

In 2021 she and Venus helped produce a film based on their own lives. *King Richard* starred Will Smith as the Williams sisters' father and focused on Venus and Serena's upbringing. The film was nominated for Best Picture at the Academy Awards. Smith won the Best Actor award.

The next year, Williams told the world that her tennis career was winding down. Instead of saying she was "retiring," Williams used the term "evolving away"

FAST FACT

Williams is an investor in Angel City FC, a team in the National Women's Soccer League. She joined more than 100 athletes and celebrities, including 13 former members of the US women's soccer team, as part owner.

from the sport, highlighting that she would continue to focus on impacting the world in other ways.

Her last tournament was the 2022 US Open. She entered unseeded, but the fans in New York hoped she had one last magical run left. Tributes poured in from everywhere. Celebrities made sure to get tickets. Broadcaster and former tennis great John McEnroe called her the "GOAT (Greatest of all Time) of GOATs." Black players like Sloane Stephens and Coco Gauff talked about how much Williams had inspired them to play. So did Osaka, who beat Williams in the 2018 US Open final.

Williams reached the third round, where she lost to Australian Ajla Tomljanović. When Williams fell behind 5–1 in the third set, the crowd at Arthur Ashe Stadium rose to give her one final ovation. Williams rewarded the crowd by saving five match points before finally losing. She thanked the crowd, then walked off as an all-time champion who had changed her sport forever, on and off the court.

Williams waves to the crowd as she exits a US Open match on Septermber 2, 2022. Before the tournament, Williams had announced she would be stepping away from the sport.

INDEX

ABOUT THE AUTHOR

Anthony K. Hewson is a freelance writer originally from San Diego. He and his wife now live in the San Francisco Bay Area with their two dogs.